Building Blocks

Math Matters!

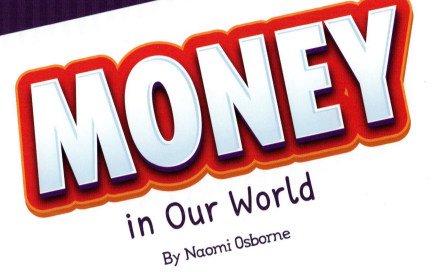

MONEY
in Our World

By Naomi Osborne

Cavendish Square

New York

We use money
to buy things.
Money is fun to count!

We count money in dollars and cents.

There are 100 cents in 1 dollar.
You can also write 1 dollar as $1.

$1

A penny is 1 cent.
There are 100 pennies
in 1 dollar.

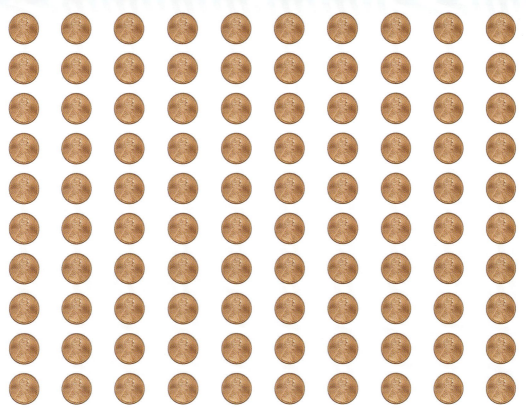

100 pennies = $1

A nickel is 5 cents.
There are 20 nickels
in 1 dollar.

20 nickels = $1

A dime is 10 cents.
There are 10 dimes
in 1 dollar.

10 dimes = $1

A quarter is 25 cents. There are 4 quarters in 1 dollar.

4 quarters = $1

A dollar bill equals $1.
Three dollar bills equals $3.

3 dollar bills = $3

You can show $5 with 5 dollar bills. You can also show it with a $5 bill.

5 dollar bills = $5

You can show $50 with 5 $10 bills. You can also show it with a $50 bill.

Five $10 bills = $50

It is fun to do math with money!

Published in 2022 by Cavendish Square Publishing, LLC
243 5th Avenue, Suite 136, New York, NY 10016

Copyright © 2022 by Cavendish Square Publishing, LLC

First Edition

No part of this publication may be reproduced, stored in a retrieval system, or transmitted in any form or by any means—electronic, mechanical, photocopying, recording, or otherwise—without the prior permission of the copyright owner. Request for permission should be addressed to Permissions, Cavendish Square Publishing, 243 5th Avenue, Suite 136, New York, NY 10016. Tel (877) 980-4450; fax (877) 980-4454.

Website: cavendishsq.com

This publication represents the opinions and views of the author based on his or her personal experience, knowledge, and research. The information in this book serves as a general guide only. The author and publisher have used their best efforts in preparing this book and disclaim liability rising directly or indirectly from the use and application of this book.

Library of Congress Cataloging-in-Publication Data

Names: Osborne, Naomi (Children's nonfiction author), author.
Title: Money in our world / Naomi Osborne.
Description: First edition. | New York : Cavendish Square Publishing, 2022. | Series: Math matters!
Identifiers: LCCN 2020007791 (print) | LCCN 2020007792 (ebook) | ISBN 9781502656599 (library binding) | ISBN 9781502656575 (paperback) | ISBN 9781502656582 (set) | ISBN 9781502656605 (ebook)
Subjects: LCSH: Money–Juvenile literature.
Classification: LCC HG221.5 .O826 2022 (print) | LCC HG221.5 (ebook) | DDC 332.4–dc23
LC record available at https://lccn.loc.gov/2020007791
LC ebook record available at https://lccn.loc.gov/2020007792

Editor: Vanessa Oswald
Copy Editor: Nathan Heidelberger
Designer: Deanna Paternostro

The photographs in this book are used by permission and through the courtesy of: Cover (top) Rrraum/Shutterstock.com; cover (bottom) Rawpixel.com/Shutterstock.com; p. 3 New Africa/Shutterstock.com; p. 5 Tamakhin Mykhailo/Shutterstock.com; pp. 7, 9 (bottom), 11 (bottom), 13 (bottom), 15 (bottom), 19 (top) nimon/Shutterstock.com; p. 9 (top) DnDavis/Shutterstock.com; pp. 11 (top), 13 (top) rsooll/Shutterstock.com; p. 15 (top) Andrey Lobachev/Shutterstock.com; p. 17 Vetal/Shutterstock.com; p. 19 (bottom) Robynrg/Shutterstock.com; p. 21 (top) stephenkirsh/Shutterstock.com; p. 21 (bottom) YamabikaY/Shutterstock.com; p. 23 People Image Studio/Shutterstock.com.

Some of the images in this book illustrate individuals who are models. The depictions do not imply actual situations or events.

CPSIA compliance information: Batch #CS22CSQ: For further information contact Cavendish Square Publishing LLC, New York, New York, at 1-877-980-4450.

Printed in the United States of America